AXOLOTL
FACT BOOK
FOR CURIOUS KIDS

170 Fascinating Facts About the
World's Most Popular Amphibian!

Astrid Hewitt

the famous axolotl smile!

Your BONUS eBooks

to download them go to

CloudberryPress.com/Axolotl

or just scan this qr code
with your phone

Contents

Introduction

Have you ever wondered what living underwater and breathing through gills would be like? **What if you could also have the superpower to regrow back any part of your body?**

Well, there is an animal that can do these things and more. *It's called an **axolotl**, and it's one of the most fascinating creatures on Earth!* Axolotls have many extraordinary abilities that make them unique.

In this book, you will learn about these wonderful animals, their history, habitat, diet, reproduction, conservation, and use in science research. You will also discover some fun facts and interesting stories about them. You will see why axolotls are so awesome and why we should protect them from extinction.

Are you ready to dive into the world of axolotls? *Then, let's get started!*

Getting to Know the Axolotl

1. What do you call these lovely creatures? They are axolotls! It's an unusual name, but it's not hard to pronounce: **ACK-suh-LAH-tuhl**

A Special Kind of Amphibian

2. The axolotl is a **salamander**! Salamanders look like lizards but are actually amphibians. Lizards are reptiles, like turtles, crocodiles, snakes, and dinosaurs. Salamanders are **amphibians**, like frogs and toads.

3. The axolotl is a special type of salamander, a paedomorphic salamander! This is just a fancy word that means axolotls look like baby salamanders their entire lives. They keep features like gills outside their bodies (usually external gills are lost when other salamanders grow up) and a long fin that goes from their head until their tails.

4. Axolotls grow up without ever going through metamorphosis. This means that the axolotl is different from most other amphibians because it does not change its body shape when it grows up.

Most amphibians, like other salamanders, frogs, and toads, start as eggs. Then, they become tadpoles with tails and no legs. And finally, they become adults and reach their final shape. **But the axolotl stays the same all its life;** it just keeps getting bigger until it becomes an adult.

Size, Weight, and Body Shape

5. An adult axolotl can measure 6 to 18 inches (15 to 45 cm). **Most axolotls are around 9 inches** (23 cm), which is close to the size of a large banana. It's rare to find axolotls that are longer than 12 inches (30 cm)

6. They are very light, weighing only 50 to 250 grams.

7. Axolotls can swim at speeds of up to 10 miles per hour (15 km/h)!

8. **Axolotls don't have eyelids**, so they can't blink or close their eyes. They sleep with their eyes open!

9. Axolotls have a very unique body shape. Their heads are wide. Their limbs are short (arms and legs) with long digits (fingers and toes). They usually have 4 digits on their front limbs and 5 on their back limbs.

10. **Axolotls have their gills OUTSIDE their bodies!** The gills are the body part that allows animals to breathe underwater. Most animals with gills (like fish) have them inside their bodies. Axolotls have 3 pairs of gill stalks.

11. Their gills are covered in tiny filaments, which look like small hairs. Each of these filaments increases the area in contact with water and helps them get more oxygen out of the water.

12. The axolotl never leaves the water, even as an adult. It keeps its gills all its life.

13. Axolotls have tiny teeth that you can barely see.

most axolotls are around this size

Colors

14. Axolotls can have many different colors! The most common ones are:

• **Wild** – Brown, or tan, with gold speckles;

• **Leucistic** – Pink with black eyes;

• **Golden Albino** – Golden with gold eyes;

• **Xhantic** – Grey with black eyes;

• **Albino** – Pale pink or white, with red eyes;

• **Melanoid** – All black or dark blue.

15. The darker-colored axolotls are often found in the wild, while the lighter ones are usually kept as pets.

16. **Some axolotls glow under black or blue light!**

Scientists created an axolotl with the *Green Fluorescent Protein* gene as an experiment. This gene was discovered in jellyfish and makes them glow green. Scientists found they could take that gene and put it into different animals. One of those animals was the axolotl!

Once a few axolotls had the gene, they could pass it to their kids. So now it's possible to find many axolotls that glow in the dark (or almost dark; you need blue or black light to see them glow)!

17. Axolotls can change their color a little bit to blend in with their environment and hide from predators!

PHOTOGRAPH BY MARCELO ALBUQUERQUE

an axolotl with the green fluorescent protein

How to Find Out If an Axolotl is a Male or Female

18. It's hard to tell if an axolotl is a male or a female until it is about one or two years old because they grow and change at different speeds. Some axolotls might show signs sooner or later than others.

19. Most of the time, you can tell if an axolotl is a male when it is about one year old. This depends on when they get a bigger **cloaca**, a part of their body near their tail, from where they poop and pee.

A male's cloaca is bigger than a female's cloaca. You can see a male's cloaca as a bump that sticks out behind its back legs, bulging from the sides.

In rare cases, you can tell if an axolotl is a boy when it is only five months old if its cloaca is already bigger than usual. But sometimes, an axolotl can be a slow grower and take as long as one and a half years to show a bigger cloaca.

20. Male axolotls usually have thinner bodies with longer tails than female axolotls.

21. While it's easy to tell if an axolotl is a male, it's not so easy to know if it's a female. **Females usually look rounder and fuller than males,** and their tails might be smaller. But this is not always true, so you can't be sure just by looking at their shape and size.

22. Sometimes you have to wait for a long time, about a year and a half, to know for sure if an axolotl is a female or not.

Sometimes, a male can look like a female when young, but then he grows up and shows his bump near his tail.

Other Curious Facts About Axolotls!

23. Even though they look very different, **axolotls are actually part of the tiger salamander family!** Tiger salamanders are usually black or brown with yellow stripes or dots.

24. Some axolotls never grow to the normal adult size. These axolotls are called "**minis**".

Minis can be as small as your hand, but they still look like normal axolotls. Sometimes, minis are small because they don't get enough food or water or because they live in a place that is too dirty or crowded.

25. Another type of small axolotl is called a "**dwarf.**"

"Dwarf" axolotls are different from minis because their bodies' shape is different from normal axolotls. They have a short and round body and a curvy tail.

They are born this way because of their genes, which are the instructions that tell their bodies how to grow.

26. *Mexican people like axolotls so much that they even drew them on their money!*

In 2021, Mexico created a new design for its banknote worth 50 pesos (the name of the money they use). The new design of the 50-peso banknote shows an axolotl swimming in the water with maize and chinampas on its back. Maize is another word for corn, and chinampas are floating gardens that people in Mexico use to grow crops on water.

The International Bank Note Society – a group of people who collect and study banknotes from around the world – liked the new design of the 50-peso banknote so much that they gave it an award called "Bank Note of the Year"!

27. **Axolotls are also sometimes called "Mexican walking fish"!**

How Do Axolotls Behave?

28. Axolotls like to stay in one place and not move much. They are happy to be in the water and watch what is happening around them.

29. They are **opportunistic hunters,** meaning that axolotls do not chase their food but wait for it to come near them.

30. They enjoy walking and swimming around the bottom of their tank when living in captivity.

31. After they eat, axolotls keep their mouths open for some time. Since their mouths have the shape of a smile, it looks like axolotls are always smiling!

32. Although they mainly use their gills to breathe, **axolotls actually have lungs and can breathe air, too!** Sometimes they will come to the water's surface and gulp some air using **"buccal pumping,"** in which they suck air in using their cheeks. This is the same method of breathing frogs and other amphibians use.

33. Sometimes axolotls get into a *"fired up"* mode and suddenly become much more active! When this happens, their bodies turn a lighter color, and their gills become a more intense red.

Some people may become worried and not understand what is happening when they see this. But this behavior is completely normal and nothing to be concerned about.

Are Axolotls Dangerous?

34. **Axolotls are very safe for people.** They usually like to be around humans and play with them as long as they're treated gently. Just don't put your fingers too close to their mouths, as they like to bite anything to check if it's edible!

35. **They're not aggressive animals but will sometimes try to defend their territory.** Especially against other axolotls.

If two axolotls fight, they can hurt each other by biting off tails, gills, and even hands or feet! This usually only happens if they live with other axolotls in a small space. Sharing a tank can, in some cases, make axolotls feel crowded and threatened.

How Do Axolotls Communicate?

36. Axolotls learn very quickly to recognize their owners, probably because they start associating humans with receiving food.

37. *Many people report that when their axolotl sees them, they swim in their direction!*

38. **Axolotls can't hear or see very well;** they move around by feeling the tiny vibrations in the water.

39. They don't have vocal cords, so they're actually mute!

40. There are videos of axolotls doing what sounds like *"barking"* or *"squeaking."* They're doing this by swallowing the air from the water's surface and

squeezing their muscles. But they're probably not doing the sounds intentionally.

41. *The only time axolotls will communicate with each other is when they want to mate.* When they want to have babies, they mostly "talk" by using their eyes and leaving behind smells in the water that other axolotls can follow.

42. **Axolotls can also feel the electrical fields that exist in the water!**

What Is the Axolotl's Natural Habitat?

43. Axolotls have only been found in one place: the freshwater lakes that used to exist under what is now Mexico City – **Lake Xochimilco** (pronounced So-Chee-Mil-Koh) and Lake Chalco.

Lake Chalco doesn't exist anymore; it was drained to prevent floods. Lake Xochimilco has almost disappeared. Its only remains are a collection of canals.

These lakes are not far from an ancient city of the Aztecs, who were a powerful people long ago. Their city was called Tenochtitlan.

44. In their natural habitat – Lake Xochimilco – the water temperature stays between 43 °F (6 °C) in the winter and 68 °F (20 °C) in the summer.

45. The word axolotl comes from the Aztec language, called Nahuatl. *Axolotl means "water animal" in the Aztec language.*

46. Axolotls used to be one of the common animals Aztecs would eat daily. Later, they were also sold as food in some markets in Mexico.

the only place in the world where
you can find wild axolotls!

The Axolotl's Life Cycle

47. Axolotls can live as long as dogs or cats. **Most axolotls in captivity live around 10 years.** However, some axolotls have lived to 15 or even 20 years in rare cases!

48. When they're in the wild, their life span is much shorter because they are vulnerable to the dangers in their natural habitat, like predators and illnesses. *In the wild, they usually live just 5 or 6 years.*

49. Once axolotls reach 6 months of age, they are ready to mate and reproduce.

Tiny Axolotl Eggs

50. An axolotl's life will start when their parents decide to breed. They usually do this during the spring season, from March to June.

51. Axolotls have a cute mating ritual in which they dance around each other in a kind of "waltz."

52. **After the mating ritual, females will lay between 300 and 1000 eggs!** Axolotl eggs are small and gelatinous (which means they look like gelatin).

53. Once a female axolotl lays eggs, they can do it again if they want to. They have the ability to restart the process again and reproduce more than one time.

PHOTOGRAPH BY KORJARIE MATIESSA

54. The eggs take two weeks to develop into tiny axolotl larvae, which look like axolotls without legs. They develop their gills, tails, and eyes before hatching (coming out of the egg).

Growing Up

55. Once they come out of the egg, they are hungry and only eat food that is alive and moving, like small worms or insects. **They need to eat many times a day during this juvenile phase.**

56. Axolotl parents don't take care of their baby axolotls. Since there are so many eggs, usually hundreds, they wouldn't be able to help everyone! After an axolotl is born, it has to care for itself and find its own food.

57. Young axolotls will get bigger quickly with enough food and water. They can grow as much as 1 or 2 inches in one month (2 to 5 cm)! When they are about 6 months old, they begin to grow more slowly.

58. When an axolotl is about 1 to one and a half years old, it will stop getting bigger. At this age, it's as big as it

will be for the rest of its life.

59. Fully grown adult axolotls do not use their energy as fast as young ones, so they don't get hungry as often. **They can go for two or three days without eating** and still be okay.

How do axolotls die?

60. **Illnesses** are one of the most common reasons an axolotl dies in the wild. They are vulnerable to many health problems, like bacteria, fungi, parasites, and sometimes cancer. Many of their illnesses are also caused by inbreeding since so few axolotls are left in the wild.

61. **Predators** are the other main reason a wild axolotl will die. Since axolotls don't have anything in their bodies to defend themselves from predators, all they can do is hide and try to swim away. This makes them obvious targets for bigger animals.

62. Axolotls even eat other axolotls! If a big axolotl can fit a smaller axolotl in its mouth, it will happily eat it.

63. **Poor care** is the main reason axolotls die in captivity. Since they need very specific conditions, they will likely become sick or hurt if their owners don't know enough about how to take care of them.

Things like not having the right kind of water, with the right temperature, having a dirty tank, or a tank that's too small can all be dangerous for an axolotl. They are very fragile, and people need to be very careful so they can live long, healthy lives.

Axolotls in Science

64. Axolotls are used by scientists as a **"model organism."** Researchers like to study many different species to learn more about how animals grow and change and why they have powers that we don't have.

They hope that if they can understand these things in animals, they can use this knowledge to help humans. They call these animals "model organisms".

Axolotls are used as a model organism and have helped us learn many things!

65. One of the reasons scientists love axolotls is that they can have many babies without much trouble, unlike their salamander "cousins" who live on land and need more intensive care to survive.

Most salamanders that live on land are not kept by scientists because they are harder to raise.

What Have We Learned from Axolotls?

66. One thing that makes the axolotl interesting for scientists is that they can see how it grows from a tiny egg to a full-grown animal with bones and muscles.

The axolotl's embryo (a word for a kind of egg) is big and soft enough that scientists can move it around and look at it from different angles.

67. Some axolotls have a gene problem that makes

their hearts stop working when they are still inside the egg.

But even though their hearts are not working, the axolotls can still live for a long time inside the egg.

Scientists use these axolotls to learn more about how hearts work and why they stop working.

68. Axolotls have also helped scientists understand how the brain and th e spine develop!

69. **Axolotls are resistant to cancer!**

70. And scientists have learned a lot about genes by watching how different combinations of genes will change the axolotl colors.

71. But the thing that makes axolotls one of the most exciting animals to study is their healing abilities! **The axolotl is an extraordinary animal that can grow back parts of its body that are cut off or damaged.**

After it heals, it does not keep any marks or scars. *It can grow back not only its legs or tail but also vital body parts like its lungs, eyes, heart, spinal cords, jaws, skin, ovaries, and even brain!*

This makes them very interesting to scientists, who love studying axolotls to understand how they can do this and if humans can learn how to do it, too.

72. Axolotls can also accept transplants from other axolotls! This means they can receive and use body parts from other axolotls, such as eyes and brain parts.

This is very interesting for scientists because when they

try this with other species, the new body parts are usually rejected, and the animals become sick.

73. Sometimes, an axolotl can grow back not only a leg or an arm that is hurt but also another one next to it. **This makes the axolotl have more legs or arms than it should!** Some people love to keep these unique axolotls as pets.

74. Axolotls are also teaching us a lot about **stem cells!** Cells are the tiny building blocks of life that are part of everything that is alive.

Most cells have their own tasks in the body. So, an eye cell only works in the eyes. But some cells are special because they can transform into any other kind of cell! These are called stem cells.

Because axolotls can grow new parts of their body using stem cells, they are very useful for learning more about how stem cells work.

75. The axolotl genome is one of the longest ever studied!

A genome is like a big book of instructions that tells every cell in your body what to do.

It is made of tiny molecules called "base pairs" that are like letters in a word. The more base pairs a genome has, the longer and more complex it is.

For a long time, scientists have wanted to read the axolotl's genome to learn how they can heal so well.

And, in 2018, they finally finished reading all 32 billion base pairs of the axolotl's genome and shared it with the world! That was a massive achievement because, at the time, it was the longest animal genome scientists had ever read.

Critically Endangered

Why Are Most of the Wild Axolotls Dying?

76. In 2020, the axolotl was considered almost extinct.

In 1998, there were around **6000** axolotls found living in the wild.

In 2003 there were only **1000.**

In 2008, only **100** were found.

And in 2013, after four months of searching, researchers only found **2.**

It's estimated that only 50 to 1000 axolotls are left, and their number is getting smaller yearly. The axolotl is on the list of animals that are considered **"critically endangered."**

77. There are 4 reasons why the wild axolotls are dying. **The first reason is that people destroyed their natural habitat.**

Axolotls have only ever lived in the Mexican Central Valley, a big land area in the middle of Mexico.

A long time ago, many axolotls were living in different places in the Mexican Central Valley. Places like lakes and wetlands. Wetlands are areas where the land is wet and muddy.

But then, people from Spain came to Mexico and took over the land from the Aztecs, who lived there before.

The Spanish people wanted to build a city, which is now called Mexico City. So, they drained the lakes and made most of the water disappear. Because of this, the majority of the axolotl's natural habitat was destroyed.

Now, very few axolotls are left, and they can only live in Lake Xochimilco because as Mexico City grew, the lakes kept getting smaller.

Nowadays, Lake Xochimilco is no longer a big lake but a collection of smaller channels, temporary wetlands, and smaller lakes.

78. **The second reason wild Axolotls are dying is bad water quality.**

Mexico City in 1690

The water in Lake Xochimilco is not healthy for the axolotls. Poor water quality can be caused by many things, but in this case, it is because people use the water for aquaculture (raising fish) and agriculture.

The water in Lake Xochimilco also comes from wastewater, which people have used for things like washing, cooking, or flushing toilets.

Wastewater is usually dirty and harmful, so it needs to be cleaned before it can be used or put back into nature. *But not all water that goes back to Lake Xochimilco gets treated, so over time, the lake got more and more polluted.*

Scientists have also done some tests on the water in Lake Xochimilco and found that the water does not have enough oxygen for the axolotls to breathe well.

79. The third reason wild Axolotls are dying is because of invasive species.

Some animals do not belong to the place where axolotls have always lived. These animals are called invasive species because they are brought by humans or arrive in some other unexpected way and invade the home of the axolotls, causing problems for them.

This is what is happening with the *Nile tilapia* and the *common carp*. These invasive fish are very hungry and greedy. **They eat the baby axolotls or their eggs before they can grow up. They also take away the food and space the axolotls need to survive.**

These fish make the axolotls scared and nervous. The axolotls try to hide and stay still so the fish do not see or attack them.

Because the axolotls hide and do not move much, they have fewer chances to find food and reproduce. Over time, this made their population smaller and weaker.

the common carp

80. The fourth reason wild Axolotls are dying is because of a loss of genetic diversity.

This means that the axolotls that live in the wild are very similar and do not have many different traits.

Since not many wild axolotls are alive anymore, the ones left are very closely related to each other, like cousins or siblings, and breed with each other more often than with unrelated axolotls. **This is called inbreeding.**

The baby axolotls born from inbreeding often inherit bad genes from their parents. This can make them sick, weak, or have problems with their bodies.

And since every new generation has more axolotls who are sick because of inbreeding, they become even more vulnerable to predators and other health problems.

Over time, these 4 reasons have made the wild axolotl almost extinct.

Why Are Wild Axolotls Important?

81. Even though axolotls are dying in the wild, **there are thousands and thousands of axolotls alive and living with people,** either as pets or in labs with researchers. *The axolotl is actually the most popular amphibian in the world!*

82. Scientists love axolotls so much that they even call them the *"white mice of amphibians"* because scientists also do a lot of experiments on white mice.

83. So, what's the problem? **Unfortunately, the axolotls that live with humans are starting to get more and more sick.**

The axolotls that live in captivity are all too similar genetically, which makes them more likely to have health problems. When there are many different genes in a group of animals, they are better at fighting off diseases and staying strong.

Since the axolotls don't have enough variety in their genes, they are not staying healthy.

84. Hoping to solve this problem, scientists have tried mixing axolotls with *tiger salamanders.*

But because of this, many of the axolotls now have genes that they wouldn't usually have, which makes them different from the axolotls that live in their natural habitat.

So, the axolotls we now have pets are no longer the same axolotls that evolved in Mexico for thousands of years. Humans changed the axolotl!

The People Trying to Save the Wild Axolotl

85. Many scientists are trying to save the axolotls by raising them in captivity and then releasing them in new places where they can live freely.

Some people are trying to reintroduce them into Lake Xochimilco, although this will probably not work until the lake gets cleaner.

86. The *Universidad Nacional Autonoma de Mexico* (UNAM) has a laboratory with more than 100 axolotls that they use for research. **They plan to create a semi-artificial wetland inside the university where the axolotls can live as if they were in the wild.** Their goal is to create a population of axolotls that can survive alone without humans caring for them.

87. Some experiments have proven that **axolotls born and raised in semi-natural environments can find and eat their own food, stay alive in the wild, and avoid predators.**

This means that these axolotls born and raised in captivity can be moved to new habitats with clean water, and they'll be able to establish a wild population that can sustain itself and live freely.

Even though this looks like an axolotl, it's actually a tiger salamander larvae!

Before going through metamorphosis, tiger salamanders look very similar to axolotls!

How to Have a Pet Axolotl

88. Axolotls have become very popular as pets! They are as popular as their "cousin," the Tiger Salamander.

89. Even though we all love this adorable amphibian, **axolotls are an advanced pet to keep because they need a lot of effort and attention.**

It's easy to forget some essential step or detail and make your axolotl dangerously sick.

They will also stay with you for 10 to 20 years. *So, only adopt an axolotl if you're willing to work hard for many years to keep it happy and healthy!*

90. **Axolotls are poikilothermic animals.** A poikilothermic animal is an animal that has a body temperature that changes with the temperature of its surroundings.

Axolotls will be cold inside their bodies if it's cold outside. If it's hot outside, they will also be hot inside.

Poikilothermic animals are different from *warm-blooded* animals, which can keep their body temperature always the same, no matter what the temperature outside is.

Humans are warm-blooded, so the temperature inside our body is always around 97 to 99 °F (36 to 37 °C). Our bodies can always keep our internal temperature in this range, even in a sauna or Antarctica!

91. When axolotls get too cold, they cannot use the energy from their food properly, and they don't feel hungry enough to eat well, so they might become sick. Owners must be careful to always keep their water at a comfortable temperature, which for axolotls is between 60 and 68 °F (15 to 20 °C).

92. Even just one day of being very cold or hot can be dangerous for an axolotl! They will often feel so stressed that they become sick and die.

93. The water from our homes' faucets, which we use to drink or shower, harms axolotls because it has a chemical called *chlorine*. Axolotls need to live in special water that is safe for fish and other aquatic animals.

94. Axolotls need a lot of space to swim and play in their tank. **Even just one axolotl needs a tank that can hold at least 40 gallons of water (around 150 liters).**

95. Axolotls usually stay near the bottom of their tank, where they can hide under rocks or plants and look for food.

96. When they're living as pets, axolotls can eat different kinds of food that humans can easily find or buy, such as small pieces of fish like salmon or trout, or different types of worms, like **earthworms, bloodworms, and waxworms.**

They can also eat small fish that are still alive, but owners should be careful because some fish might come with parasites (tiny creatures inside them that can harm the axolotls).

97. Choosing the right **substrate** (the stuff that covers the bottom of the tank) is very important because

axolotls sometimes swallow things by accident when they eat their food, which can cause problems in their stomachs and intestines. They sometimes even die because of this!

For this reason, when people take care of axolotls, they should never keep anything smaller than the axolotl's head to ensure they won't eat it by accident.

although it looks pretty, most pebbles in this substrate are too small and should be avoided!

What Do Axolotls Eat?

98. The axolotl is a carnivorous animal. In the wild, they eat almost anything they can find and suck into their mouths. Things like:

• **Small mollusks** — Which are animals from the same family as clams, snails, slugs, squids, and octopus.

• **Worms** — They love earthworms, bloodworms, mealworms, blackworms, and wax worms.

• **Insects and other Arthropods** — And insect larvae like the mosquito larvae.

99. *They use suction to capture their food when they want to eat.* They suck water along with prey into their mouths!

Healthy Food for Pet Axolotls

100. The perfect day-to-day healthy foods for axolotls are earthworms and nightcrawlers.

These worms have all the nutrients that an axolotl needs. They are mostly made of *protein* — which helps build muscles and bones — and have the right amount of *calcium* and *phosphorus*, essential minerals for an axolotl's body.

They are also very easy to find in many stores because people sell them for fishing or feeding other animals.

earthworms

101. Axolotl keepers usually also grow their own worms at home by creating a special place for them to live and giving them food scraps. This is called a **"worm farm"**. This way, they can save money and always have fresh worms for their axolotl.

102. Besides giving axolotls worms, people also give them *fish pellets*. These are small round pieces of food that are made especially for axolotls.

Delicious Treats for Axolotls

103. Sometimes, owners give axolotls yummy snacks, like small frozen worms or gels made from insects. But these snacks should not be offered too often, because they do not have all the vitamins and minerals that axolotls need to be healthy!

104. **Some of the axolotls' favorite treats are frozen bloodworms, waxworms, and blackworms.**

105. Many axolotl owners also like to give their axolotl some small *cherry shrimp* or *ghost shrimp*, still alive. This way, the axolotl can try to hunt their snacks!

But they must be careful because some shrimp have germs or bugs that make axolotls sick. For this reason, many owners also raise their own shrimp to make sure it's healthy.

When shrimps are bought from a store, they should be kept in a separate tank for a month and given medicine to ensure they are clean and healthy before they meet an axolotl!

Foods That Axolotls Can't Eat!

106. Many people like to give axolotls fish that are alive so the axolotls can hunt them and eat them.

But some fish – like **goldfish** and **minnows** – have a substance in their bodies called *thiaminase* that can make axolotls sick if they eat it too often.

So, axolotls should not eat fish like goldfish or minnows!

107. *Some other live fish can bite an axolotl's gills and skin, hurting them and making them vulnerable to infections.* Fish from pet stores can also carry germs and parasites that can make an axolotl sick or even kill them. Many of these fish also need warmer water to live, so they can't be in the cold water that axolotls need.

goldfish

Tank Mates

108. **Axolotls are a solitary species.** We, as humans, feel sad and lonely if we're alone for too long. But axolotls are different. They don't need to be around other axolotls. **They don't make friends and never feel lonely.**

109. Sometimes, axolotls might get close to each other, but this is usually random. Unless they're trying to mate or eat each other, axolotls rarely interact.

110. *Having more than one axolotl in the same tank doesn't make them healthier or happier and can actually be risky.* At best, they probably feel neutral about it. But in some cases, it might even be worse because they might think the other axolotl is food and try to eat it.

If one axolotl's head can fit inside the other's mouth, the bigger one might try to swallow the smaller one whole!

Or they might mate and lay eggs you don't want or can't take care of.

Having more than one axolotl will also make the water dirty much faster, which can be unhealthy for themselves and other animals.

111. Apart from giving it as food, some owners may also put ghost or cherry shrimps in the same water tank to help eat the leftover food and waste the axolotls make.

But the axolotls will probably think the shrimps are just food and try to eat them.

Because of this, it's better to wait until an axolotl is at least 6 inches (15 cm) before you put any shrimps in the same tank. **If the axolotl is too small, it may have trouble swallowing and digesting the shrimp.**

112. Shrimp is the safest option for a tank mate, assuming an axolotl is big enough. They won't bother the axolotl; in the worst-case scenario, the axolotl will just eat them, which is not a problem.

113. **If you want your axolotl to have another axolotl as a tank mate, you need to keep the new axolotl in a different tank for at least a month.** This is because it might have parasites or diseases that can make your axolotl sick. Before letting them live together, you must check if the new axolotl is healthy and clean.

Some parasites can even take longer than a month to show any symptoms! So you need to be very careful and watch your new friend closely for any changes or problems. *If you see anything wrong, you should take them to a vet or an expert who can help them.*

114. If you have more than one axolotl in your aquarium, **you need to make sure they eat in different places.** Otherwise, they might hurt each other by accident.

115. Axolotls learn quickly to associate humans with food. So, when your axolotl sees you, it thinks it's time to eat! Over time, this will make them immediately start nipping anything around them. This can be a problem if other animals or plants are in the tank.

having too many axolotls together can make them feel stressed

What if they accidentally lay eggs?

116. When young axolotls live together in the same tank, there's a high chance that one will be male and the other female. If this happens, they will mate.

If you're not trying to breed axolotls, this will be a problem. The female axolotl will lay *hundreds of eggs* in the water, and you will have to remove them from the tank, or they will hatch int

117. Axolotl eggs from unknown parents and grandparents should never be raised!

This is because the axolotls that live with humans – as pets or for research – suffer from many genetic diseases. These are diseases that parents can pass on to their kids.

So, it's very important that we only raise axolotls from parents that we know for sure don't have any dangerous genes.

118. If axolotls lay eggs by mistake, the correct thing to do is put the eggs in the freezer so they can die peacefully. This is not ideal, but it's better than letting them hatch and suffer from diseases or deformities.

119. This is why we should only let people who know what they are doing make more axolotls. They can keep track of the family trees and make sure they only breed axolotls with good genes. **These people are called ethical breeders, and if you ever buy an axolotl, you should make sure you buy it from an ethical breeder.**

120. **Ethical breeders** are also careful not to let a female axolotl lay eggs more than twice a year. Having babies is hard work for her body, and she needs time to rest and recover. If she has babies too often, she might get tired or sick, and her babies might not be healthy.

How to Turn an Aquarium into a Cozy Home for an Axolotl

121. An axolotl needs a lot of water to feel good! You need **at least 29 gallons of water** in your aquarium (110 liters) for each axolotl you have. This is the smallest amount of water they can live in, but they would be happier with more.

122. **When you choose a tank for your axolotl, you should pick one that is long and wide, not tall and narrow,** because axolotls like to wander around the bottom of the tank and don't swim up too much.

123. Even though it's possible to keep an axolotl in a 29-gallon tank, the bigger the tank, the better! **Most people choose to have them in 40-gallon tanks (180 liters)** so they have enough space and water to feel comfortable.

124. *Young axolotls grow very fast,* so you can't use a smaller aquarium for them and then move them to a bigger one later. They need a big aquarium from the start because they will quickly outgrow a small one.

125. Axolotls poop a lot, and their poop makes the water dirty with something called **nitrate.**

The water in the tank gets more and more nitrate daily, and we must keep it low by changing some of the water regularly. Otherwise, the axolotls will feel very unhappy and sick. The nitrate level should always be below 20 ppm (you need a special test kit to tell you this number).

Bigger tanks with more water are better also because it will take longer for the nitrate level to rise, so you don't need to change the water as often.

126. *Sometimes axolotls can accidentally jump out of their aquariums if there is too much water in it!*

You can stop axolotls from jumping out by not filling the tank with too much water or by putting a lid or something else on top of the tank. You have to be careful with lids made of metal, though, as they might get rusty and make the water dirty.

sand is safe!

What Should You Put on the Bottom of Your Tank?

127. **If you put gravel (a word for small rocks) on the bottom of your axolotl's home, they might accidentally swallow it and get sick.** Often, these rocks get stuck in their belly, and they can't poop it out. We call this **impaction**, and it can be a dangerous thing for an axolotl.

128. You should not put anything in an axolotl's home that is small enough for them to fit in their mouth. They might think it is food and try to eat it, but it could hurt them or make them choke. **Everything around them should be bigger than their heads.**

129. If you want to use sand on the bottom of your axolotl's home, you should choose the smooth and tiny kind. This way, **if your axolotl swallows some sand, it can easily pass through their body without causing any trouble.**

However, even sand can cause problems for young axolotls because they're still too small for sand to pass through them.

Once an axolotl grows to 6 inches (15 cm), it's big enough to be around sand safely.

130. Instead of using sand or gravel on the bottom of your axolotl's home, you can use some big rocks that your axolotl can't fit in their mouth. This way, you can avoid the risk of **impaction** and keep your axolotl happy and safe.

131. Another option is to leave the bottom of your axolotl's tank empty. This can be good because you can clean it more efficiently by removing any dirt or waste that accumulates there.

But your axolotl may have a harder time moving around or staying in one place because there is nothing to hold on to with their feet.

132. If you think that leaving the bottom of the tank empty looks boring, you can decorate it with some tiles! Just make sure they haven't been treated with chemicals or paints that could harm your axolotl.

rocks bigger than the axolot's head are also a safe choice!

How to Decorate Your Axolotl's Aquarium

133. **It's important to give your axolotl a home with enough variety of plants and hiding spots so they can feel comfortable and happy.**

135. Some axolotls like to play with the tiny bubbles that come out of a device called an air stone. An air stone is something that you put in the tank to make sure the water has enough oxygen. Some axolotls may try to catch the bubbles or swim through them for fun.

137. **Putting real plants in the tank with your axolotl is also possible.** Live plants can make the tank look more natural and beautiful.

138. *Remember that axolotls don't have eyelids! They can't close their eyes, so too much light can stress them.* You should be careful about how bright you make their tank.

139. This means you should choose plants that don't need much light or warmth to grow. Some examples of these plants are:

• **Elodeas**

• **Anubias**

• **Java ferns**

• **Java moss**

• **Marimo algae balls,** which are round green balls of algae (as long as they're bigger than the axolotl's head!);

...but there are many more to choose from!

These plants can live happily in low light and cold water with your axolotl.

136. You can change how the things in the tank are arranged occasionally to make it more interesting for your axolotl. **You can move the hiding spots, plants, or other decorations around to create a new look for the tank.** Your axolotl will enjoy discovering the new places in its home.

134. You should put some things in the tank that your axolotl can go inside or behind when it wants to be alone or feel safe.

You can use rocks, caves, pipes, or plants to make hiding spots for your axolotl. Your axolotl will like having different places to explore and rest in its tank.

axolotls like to hide!

Advanced Skills Needed to Have a Pet Axolotl

140. **Having pet axolotls is a lot of fun, but there are many complex skills you need to have to make sure they survive and stay healthy!** If you decide to have a pet axolotl, you'll need someone to help you learn and practice these essential tasks.

Cycling Your Aquarium

141. **Cycling an aquarium means growing some good bacteria colonies inside your tank.** Bacteria are tiny living things that can only be seen with a microscope. These bacteria colonies will help keep the water clean and healthy for your axolotl.

142. **Every animal that lives in water, like axolotls, or fish, makes a chemical called ammonia when they poop or pee.** Ammonia is very bad for them and can make them sick. The good bacteria can eat the ammonia and turn it into a chemical called nitrite, then into another called **nitrate**. *Nitrate is not as bad as ammonia, but it still needs to be removed through regular water changes.*

143. You need to ensure that the good bacteria are living in your tank before you put an axolotl or other animals in it. **If you don't do this, they might get sick and die from the ammonia.**

144. Cycling an aquarium is a complicated process with many steps! **You'll need the help of someone who has done it before to make sure everything is working correctly.**

145. Cycling your aquarium will take at least a month, and only after that will the aquarium be safe for axolotls!

Measuring the Water Quality

146. Axolotls can only live in water with a precise amount of chemicals. The only way to know how much of these chemicals are in the water is to measure it and write down the numbers. We call these the **water parameters.**

147. **It's impossible to know if an axolotl is healthy just by looking at them, so it's essential to always know the water parameters!** That's the only way to tell if your axolotl is happy or stressed. Water can become toxic quickly if an axolotl owner does not regularly check the water quality.

You can buy water test kits to measure these parameters.

Water Changes

148. **Every week, you'll need to change part of the water in the tank to remove the excess nitrate that will accumulate over time.**

149. You'll need to add a **water conditioner** when you change the water. Water conditioners are substances that make the new water safe for your axolotl.

Water often contains chemicals like chlorine an chloramine, which kill harmful bacteria and viruses. However, these chemicals also harm axolotls, fish, and plants.

Water conditioners react with these chemicals and turn them into harmless substances.

150. Many water conditioners contain **aloe vera.** *Aloe vera is actually an irritant to axolotls!* It makes them uncomfortable and might cause them pain. So always use a conditioner without aloe vera!

Water Temperature

151. **Keeping the water temperature between 60 to 68 °F (15 to 20 °C) is extremely important.**

If the water temperature is outside this range, your axolotl will quickly become stressed, sick, and might even die!

152. To ensure the water temperature stays at healthy levels for axolotls, you'll need an accurate **thermometer** and a good method to heat or cool the water.

Usually, you won't need to heat the water up. Most people don't keep their homes below 60 °F (15 °C), so the water will probably not become too cold.

But during hot summer days, there's a risk the water will become too warm! So, it's essential to have an effective way to make the water colder.

The best methods are:

153. **A water chiller** – These are machines that are outside the tank. The water from the tank goes into the chiller and comes out colder. Then, it goes back to the tank.

Water chillers are the best way to keep the water always at the right temperature. Unfortunately, they are also very expensive.

154. **Fans blowing air over the water** – This method is much cheaper and can lower the water temperature by up to 6°F (3 °C). But it doesn't work on the hottest days.

155. **Adding ice to the water** – *This method is not a good permanent solution* because you would always need to be close to the aquarium, checking the water temperature and adding more ice. But it's a good method to use during emergencies.

156. As with the other advanced skills, keeping the water at the right temperature can be complicated, so you'll need the help of someone with experience to ensure your axolotl will always be safe.

What If Your Axolotl Gets Sick?

157. Axolotls will sometimes get sick, and it can be hard to understand what's happening. **If you think your axolotl is ill, you should take it to the vet as soon as possible!**

158. Here is a list of signs to look out for:

- *Folded gills*

- *Folded tail*

- *Red marks on the skin*

- *Small pieces of skin seem to be falling off*

- *Gills seem smaller, or little pieces are falling off*

- *They're constantly scratching themselves*

- *White patches on the body or gills (could be a fungus)*

- *Cuts and scratches (might cause an infection)*

- *Not eating the same amounts of food as usual*

- *Floating close to the water's surface for too long*

- *Swollen body parts*

159. If your pet axolotl shows one or more of these signs, the best thing to do is talk to a vet with experience treating axolotls!

Metamorphosis

160. **Even though it's rare, axolotls can go through metamorphosis too!**

Most amphibians, like frogs and salamanders, start as little creatures that look like fish and can only breathe underwater. *During this phase of their lives, we call them tadpoles.*

When they grow up, their bodies completely change their shape. This is called metamorphosis (which is a word that means to change or transform).

They stop having gills, the body parts that let them breathe underwater, and they start having lungs, the organs that allow them to breathe air. They also grow legs and arms and sometimes change their colors, too. *Then, they can hop out of the water and live on land.*

The axolotl is very different from other amphibians. It does not have enough of a particular chemical in its body, called thyroid stimulating hormone, which tells its thyroid (a part of its brain) to make something called **thyroxine**.

Thyroxine is what makes other amphibians change their bodies when they grow up. But because the axolotl does not have enough of it, its body never changes. It keeps its gills and stays in the water all its life, even as an adult.

161. **The axolotl's body can still undergo metamorphosis if it gets this chemical from somewhere else,** such as a scientist who gives it a shot or puts it in its water.

This is not a natural process but an artificial one (made by humans). **When this happens, the axolotl changes its body like other amphibians and starts living on land instead of water.**

162. One way that humans can make axolotls change their bodies is by giving them an injection of a substance called iodine. Iodine helps the thyroid produce the chemicals that tell the body to change. **When axolotls get iodine in their bodies, they can go through metamorphosis too.**

163. *Even though it's possible to make axolotls go through metamorphosis with this method, it's very dangerous, and many die.* For this reason, it's never recommended that owners try to do it with their pets.

164. Sometimes, very rarely, some axolotls go through metamorphosis without humans doing anything! They just have some genes that make them morph once they reach 5 to 10 months of age.

When this happens to a pet axolotl, their owners have to move them out of the aquarium and create a new home for them since they lose their gills and can no longer breathe underwater.

165. **When an axolotl goes through metamorphosis, its body changes in many different ways:**

• **It makes its legs stronger and more flexible** *so it can walk and run on land.*

• **The gills and fins are absorbed by its body** *and disappear since it doesn't need them to breathe water or swim anymore.*

• **It grows eyelids** *so it can blink and protect its eyes from dust and dirt.*

• **It makes its skin less leaky,** *so it doesn't lose water from its body when it is dry outside.*

• **It makes its lungs bigger** *and better to be able to breathe air more efficiently.*

166. An axolotl that has undergone metamorphosis becomes very similar to the Mexican Tiger Salamander, the main difference being that it has longer toes.

167. **When the axolotl goes through metamorphosis, it loses some of its power to grow back parts of its body. It can still heal, but not as well as before.**

168. *If you ever get a pet axolotl that goes through metamorphosis accidentally, you should contact its breeder as soon as possible!*

This is important because when people buy an axolotl, they expect to have an aquatic pet for the next 10 or 15 years.

If the axolotl morphs and becomes a land animal, it's a big surprise! Most people don't know how to take care of this new terrestrial salamander. They need a different habitat, are difficult to feed, and become stressed easily.

For these reasons, the breeder should be contacted so they know which parents have the metamorphosis genes. This way, they can retire the parents and not let them lay any more eggs.

a morphed axolotl - looks very similar to a tiger salamander

The Amazing Axolotl Myth

169. **The Aztecs have an extraordinary story about how axolotls came to exist.** They believed that the sun was stuck in the sky and it would only move when someone was sacrificed. *This means someone would have to die for the sun to move.* In their stories, the first ones to be sacrificed were the gods.

Xolotl was one of the gods the Aztecs believed in. He was their god of fire and lightning. And the god Xolotl didn't want to die! So, he decided to hide by changing himself into other forms.

• **First, he changed himself into the maize plant.** And that's why the Aztec word for corn is *xolotl*.

• **Second, he changed into the agave plant.** So the Aztec word for agave is *mexolotl*.

• **Finally, he changed himself into the "water animal."** And so, this little animal became known as the *axolotl!*

170. According to the myth, Xolotl was finally found by his brother Quetzalcoatl. His brother decided not to sacrifice Xolotl to the sun, but as punishment for trying to hide, *he made him live forever in the darkness as an axolotl.*

And so, the Aztecs believed that all "water animals" contain the spirit of Xolotl. In a way, each axolotl is a little god!

an ancient statue
of the god Xolotl

Conclusion

We've reached the end of our book, and I hope you enjoyed learning about this wonderful amphibian!

You've learned about the unique ways axolotls are different from other salamanders. *About its size and shape, its colors, and all the ways it's being studied by scientists to help us learn about its magical healing abilities!*

You now understand why axolotls are important and why they're disappearing from their original habitat.

If you decide to have a pet axolotl, you've learned what it takes to make sure they live a happy and healthy life!

Axolotls are definitely one of the most incredible animals we have ever discovered. And you now know more about axolotls than most people in the world!

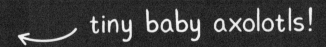 tiny baby axolotls!